Airbnb Essentials

Latest Strategies
to Build a Successful Business

Ghazwan Alemara

Contents

Introduction

Imagine being able to open your door to travelers from around the world, offering them a unique space and experience, while also earning extra income. Whether it's a cozy apartment, a charming guesthouse, or a vacation home, Airbnb has revolutionized the way we share our spaces and connect with people from all walks of life. Hosting on Airbnb has become more than just a way to make money—it's an opportunity to become a part of someone's journey, to create memorable stays, and to build a profitable side business on your terms.

This book is your comprehensive guide to mastering the art of Airbnb hosting. In a world where flexibility and personalized experiences are increasingly valued, Airbnb allows you to turn your space into an income-generating asset while also providing a unique experience for your guests. As a host, you have the power to craft an environment that stands out, meets guest expectations, and leaves a lasting impression. But to truly succeed, there's more to it than simply listing your property. This book will walk you through each step, equipping you with the tools, insights, and strategies to become an exceptional host.

The purpose of this book is simple: to help you maximize the potential of your property and deliver unforgettable stays for your guests. Whether you're a new host eager to get started or an experienced one looking to refine your approach, this book is designed to provide you with practical, actionable advice on every aspect of hosting. From preparing your space and setting competitive prices to understanding local regulations and building positive guest relationships, you'll gain insights that will not only help you attract more bookings but also ensure a rewarding experience for you and your guests.

In today's travel landscape, more people are seeking out unique, personal, and memorable experiences. As travelers increasingly opt for Airbnb over traditional hotels, the opportunity for hosts to stand out and succeed has never been greater. However, with this opportunity comes the responsibility of meeting guest expectations, providing a safe and clean environment, and managing your property effectively. This book addresses these challenges, offering solutions and strategies tailored to the Airbnb platform and today's hosting landscape.

The book is structured to guide you through every stage of the hosting journey, with chapters covering essential topics such as preparing your property, managing your listing, communicating with guests, and handling finances and regulations. Each chapter is packed with insights and practical steps to help you navigate the nuances of Airbnb hosting and elevate your guest experience. By the end, you'll have a well-rounded understanding of how to create a welcoming, profitable, and successful Airbnb property.

With a straightforward and engaging tone, this book aims to make the process of hosting on Airbnb accessible and enjoyable. You'll find the advice easy to follow, with real-world examples and tips that are immediately applicable. Whether your goal is to turn your hosting into a full-time business or simply make the most of an extra space, this guide will provide the knowledge and confidence you need.

Ready to transform your space into a sought-after destination? Dive in, and let's explore the possibilities that Airbnb hosting offers. Together, we'll unlock the strategies, insights, and best practices that will help you make the most of your hosting experience and build a successful Airbnb business.

Chapter 1: Introduction to Airbnb Hosting and Staying

The Rise of Airbnb: A Brief History

Airbnb began as a simple idea to help people find affordable lodging and allow homeowners to earn extra income. The story of Airbnb starts in 2008, when two roommates, Brian Chesky and Joe Gebbia, were struggling to pay rent in San Francisco. During a design conference that caused hotels to fill up, they saw an opportunity. They decided to rent out air mattresses in their apartment to attendees who couldn't find accommodation, offering them breakfast and local tips. This small venture was the seed that would grow into Airbnb.

Encouraged by their initial success, Chesky and Gebbia teamed up with Nathan Blecharczyk, and together they developed a website to connect hosts with guests. They called it "AirBed & Breakfast." The platform allowed anyone with a spare room, a couch, or an air mattress to list their space and offer it to travelers. The idea was revolutionary: it created a community-driven marketplace that was both flexible and affordable.

The early days of Airbnb were challenging. The founders had to convince people that staying in a stranger's home was safe and enjoyable. They faced skepticism and financial hurdles, but they persevered. A pivotal moment came in 2009 when Airbnb received funding from Y Combinator, a startup accelerator. This investment provided the resources needed to improve their platform and expand their reach.

Airbnb's growth was rapid. By 2011, the platform had over one million nights booked. The company rebranded to "Airbnb," dropping the "AirBed & Breakfast" to reflect a broader range of accommodations. They expanded internationally, opening offices around the world and adapting their services to various cultures and markets.

One of the key factors in Airbnb's success was its ability to create trust between hosts and guests. The introduction of features like user reviews, secure payment systems, and a host guarantee program helped build confidence. Additionally, Airbnb offered 24/7 customer support, ensuring that both hosts and guests felt supported throughout their experience.

As the platform grew, so did the variety of listings. Airbnb became known not just for affordable stays but for unique and diverse accommodations. From treehouses and yurts to luxurious villas and urban apartments, there was something for everyone. This variety attracted a wide range of travelers, from budget-conscious backpackers to families and business professionals.

Airbnb also tapped into the trend of experiential travel. They introduced "Airbnb Experiences" in 2016, allowing hosts to offer activities and tours, showcasing their local culture and expertise. This addition transformed Airbnb from a simple lodging platform into a comprehensive travel ecosystem.

Today, Airbnb operates in over 220 countries and regions, with millions of listings worldwide. It has revolutionized the travel industry by offering a more personal, flexible, and affordable alternative to traditional hotels. The platform continues to evolve, constantly introducing new features and services to enhance the user experience.

The rise of Airbnb is a testament to the power of innovation and community. It has redefined the way we travel and connect with others, making the world feel a little smaller and more accessible. As we explore the essentials of hosting and staying with Airbnb, it's important to appreciate the journey that brought us here and the possibilities that lie ahead.

The Host's Role in Airbnb's Success

Airbnb's remarkable ascent in the hospitality industry is not solely attributed to its innovative platform but significantly to the hosts who bring it to life. As a host, you are the cornerstone of Airbnb's success, transforming the concept of home-sharing into a global phenomenon that reshapes how people travel and experience new places.

Creating Unique and Memorable Experiences

At the heart of Airbnb's appeal is the unique and personalized experiences that hosts offer. Unlike traditional accommodations, Airbnb allows travelers to immerse themselves in local cultures, neighborhoods, and homes that reflect the authentic character of a destination. As a host, you curate these experiences by infusing your personality, style, and local knowledge into your space. Your attention to detail from interior décor to the little touches that make guests feel welcome, elevates a simple stay into a memorable journey.

By offering more than just a place to sleep, you create connections and stories that guests carry with them long after they leave. These positive experiences not only foster repeat visits but also encourage guests to share their stories with others, amplifying Airbnb's reach through word-of-mouth and reviews.

Building Trust and Community

Trust is a fundamental element of Airbnb's model, and hosts play a pivotal role in establishing and maintaining it. By providing safe, clean, and comfortable accommodations, you assure guests that they can rely on Airbnb for their travel needs. Prompt communication, transparency in listings, and honesty in interactions build a rapport with guests that is essential for a thriving community.

Moreover, hosts often become ambassadors of their local areas, offering insider tips, recommendations, and guidance that enrich the guest experience. This personal connection fosters a sense of community between hosts and travelers, distinguishing Airbnb from impersonal hotel stays.

Driving Innovation and Growth

Hosts contribute to Airbnb's continuous innovation by adapting to guest needs and market trends. Your feedback, creativity, and willingness to try new approaches help the platform evolve. Whether it's adopting sustainable practices, implementing smart home technologies, or experimenting with unique space designs, hosts are at the forefront of enhancing the Airbnb experience.

By staying responsive to guest preferences and industry developments, you not only improve your own hosting success but also contribute to the collective growth of the Airbnb community. Your innovations become part of the shared knowledge that other hosts can learn from, creating a dynamic environment where everyone benefits.

Economic Impact and Empowerment

Hosting on Airbnb empowers individuals to generate additional income, supporting personal financial goals and fostering entrepreneurship. For many, it provides the flexibility to pursue passions, invest in property improvements, or support families. On a larger scale, hosts contribute to local economies by attracting travelers who spend money at nearby businesses, restaurants, and attractions.

This economic impact extends beyond individual hosts to communities and cities, promoting tourism and cultural exchange. By participating in Airbnb, you become a vital part of an ecosystem that stimulates growth and development in your area.

Upholding Airbnb's Reputation

The collective efforts of hosts shape Airbnb's global reputation. Consistently delivering high-quality experiences ensures that guests trust and choose Airbnb for their travels. Your commitment to excellence reflects on the platform as a whole, influencing guest perceptions and decisions.

Negative experiences can impact not only individual hosts but also the broader community. Therefore, maintaining high standards in hospitality, adhering to policies, and striving for positive reviews are essential responsibilities. By upholding Airbnb's values and guidelines, you protect and enhance the platform's reputation.

Embracing the Role of a Host

Being an Airbnb host is more than renting out a space—it's about hospitality, connection, and contribution. You have the opportunity to make a difference in the lives of travelers, offering them comfort, insight, and memorable experiences. Embrace this role with enthusiasm and professionalism, knowing that your efforts are integral to Airbnb's ongoing success.

As you continue your hosting journey, remember that every interaction counts. Your dedication to creating exceptional stays not only benefits your own endeavors but also strengthens the entire Airbnb community. Together, hosts like you are redefining hospitality and shaping the future of travel.

Why Choose Airbnb? Benefits for Hosts and Guests

Airbnb has revolutionized the travel and hospitality industry by offering an alternative to traditional hotels. But what makes it so appealing? The benefits for both hosts and guests are numerous and compelling, making Airbnb a preferred choice for many.

For hosts, Airbnb provides a flexible and lucrative way to earn extra income. Whether you have a spare room, a vacation home, or even your primary residence available for short-term rental, Airbnb allows you to monetize your space. This extra income can help cover mortgage payments, fund travel, or simply provide additional financial security. Hosting on Airbnb also offers a unique opportunity to meet new people from around the world. Many hosts find joy in sharing their homes and local knowledge with travelers, creating a sense of community and connection that is often missing in other forms of rental.

In addition to financial benefits, hosts have the flexibility to rent out their space according to their own schedule. You can decide when to make your home available and block off dates when you want to keep it for personal use. This level of control makes Airbnb an attractive option compared to long-term rentals, which require more permanent commitments.

Guests, on the other hand, are drawn to Airbnb for the variety and uniqueness of accommodations available. Unlike the uniformity of hotel rooms, Airbnb offers a diverse range of places to stay, from chic city apartments to rustic countryside cottages. This variety allows travelers to find a space that perfectly fits their needs and preferences. Often, staying in an Airbnb can provide a more authentic and immersive travel experience. Guests can live like locals, staying in residential neighborhoods and enjoying a more personalized and homey atmosphere.

Another significant advantage for guests is the potential for cost savings. Airbnb accommodations can often be more affordable than hotels, especially for longer stays or larger groups. Many listings offer amenities like kitchens and laundry facilities, which can help travelers save on dining out and laundry services. Additionally, guests often appreciate the personal touches that hosts provide, such as local tips, welcome snacks, or even guided tours of the area.

Airbnb's platform also emphasizes safety and trust. Both hosts and guests can read reviews and ratings before making a booking decision, ensuring a level of transparency and reliability. This mutual review system helps maintain high standards and build trust within the Airbnb community.

For those concerned about safety and security, Airbnb provides various measures to protect both hosts and guests. Hosts can verify the identity of their guests and set house rules to ensure their property is respected. Guests, too, can feel secure knowing that their host has been reviewed by previous travelers and that they have a clear understanding of the accommodation's rules and expectations.

Overall, Airbnb offers a win-win solution for hosts and guests. It creates opportunities for financial gain, cultural exchange, and unique travel experiences. Whether you're looking to generate extra income by sharing your space or seeking a memorable and cost-effective place to stay, Airbnb provides a platform that benefits everyone involved.

Chapter 2: Preparing Your Space for Guests

Decluttering and Cleaning: Creating a Welcoming Environment

Creating a welcoming environment is the first step to becoming a successful Airbnb host. The foundation of a great guest experience is a clean, clutter-free space where create a welcoming environment that sets a professional tone, making guests feel comfortable while showing that you, as a host, care about their experience. This section will guide you through the essentials of decluttering and cleaning, ensuring your space is always ready to impress.

Example of a Room Setup. Source: gretchenkamp.com.

Decluttering: Less is More

A clutter-free space not only looks more inviting but also helps guests feel at ease. Start by assessing each room with a critical eye. Remove items that are not essential or that could potentially make the space feel crowded. This doesn't mean your home has to be sparse or devoid of personality, but aim for a balance between functional and decorative items.

Consider your guests' needs and prioritize those. Provide clear surfaces on tables, desks, and counters so guests have room for their belongings. Closets and storage areas should have ample space for guests to unpack and store their items. If you're storing personal items in the space, ensure they are neatly organized and out of sight.

Decluttering also involves simplifying your decor. Opt for a few tasteful, well-placed items rather than a collection of knick-knacks. This approach not only makes cleaning easier but also prevents the space from feeling overwhelming.

Cleaning: A Sparkling First Impression

A clean space is non-negotiable for any successful Airbnb. Guests expect a level of cleanliness that rivals hotels, and it's your responsibility to meet or exceed those expectations. Begin with a thorough deep clean of your entire space. This sets the standard for the level of cleanliness you'll maintain between guest stays.

In the kitchen, ensure all surfaces, appliances, and utensils are spotless. Pay special attention to areas like the fridge, oven, and microwave, which can easily be overlooked but are critical for a good impression. Provide clean dish towels, sponges, and dishwashing supplies.

The bathroom is another high-priority area. Scrub all surfaces, including the toilet, sink, and shower or bathtub. Ensure mirrors and fixtures are gleaming. Replace used towels with fresh, fluffy ones and stock up on essential toiletries such as soap, shampoo, and toilet paper.

In the bedroom, focus on clean linens and an inviting bed. Wash and change sheets, pillowcases, and duvet covers between each guest. Dust all surfaces and vacuum the floors, ensuring no corner is neglected. Providing extra blankets and pillows in a neat and accessible manner is a nice touch.

Living areas should be dusted, vacuumed, and organized. Clean upholstery and rugs, and fluff up any throw pillows or cushions. Wipe down all surfaces, including electronics and light fixtures, to ensure there are no fingerprints or dust.

Maintenance Cleaning: Keeping It Up

Maintaining cleanliness between guest stays is crucial. Develop a cleaning checklist that covers all areas of your space and follow it rigorously. This ensures nothing is missed and maintains the high standard of cleanliness your guests expect.

Invest in quality cleaning supplies and tools to make your job easier. A good vacuum, microfiber cloths, and effective cleaning solutions can make a significant difference. If managing cleaning on your own becomes too demanding, consider hiring a professional cleaning service to help.

Pay attention to small details. Refill toiletries, restock kitchen supplies, and replace any damaged or worn items promptly. Fresh flowers, a small welcome note, or a local treat can add a personal touch that makes guests feel special and appreciated.

Final Touches: Creating an Inviting Atmosphere

Once your space is clean and decluttered, think about the little extras that can enhance the atmosphere. Soft lighting, pleasant scents, and comfortable furnishings all contribute to a welcoming environment. Open windows to let in fresh air before guests arrive, and ensure the temperature is comfortable.

Creating a welcoming environment through effective decluttering and thorough cleaning sets the stage for a positive guest experience. When guests walk into a spotless, well-organized space, they can immediately relax and start enjoying their stay. Your attention to detail and commitment to cleanliness will not only lead to happy guests but also to glowing reviews and repeat bookings.

Safety First: Must-Have Safety Features

Ensuring the safety of your guests is paramount to providing a comfortable and reliable Airbnb experience. A safe environment not only protects your guests but also gives them peace of mind during their stay. Here, we will discuss the essential safety features every Airbnb should have.

Smoke and Carbon Monoxide Detectors

One of the most critical safety features in any home is a working smoke detector. Install smoke detectors in key areas such as the kitchen, bedrooms, and hallways. Regularly test them to ensure they are functioning correctly and replace the batteries at least once a year.

In addition to smoke detectors, carbon monoxide detectors are equally important, especially if you have gas appliances. Carbon monoxide is an odorless, colorless gas that can be deadly. Place detectors near sleeping areas and any gas appliances, and check them regularly to ensure they are operational.

Fire Extinguishers

Having a fire extinguisher readily available can prevent a small fire from becoming a disaster. Place fire extinguishers in the kitchen and near any potential fire hazards. Ensure they are easily accessible and that guests know their locations. Regularly check the expiration dates and replace extinguishers as needed.

First Aid Kit

A well-stocked first aid kit is a must for any Airbnb. Include basic items such as bandages, antiseptic wipes, adhesive tape, scissors, tweezers, and pain relievers. Place the first aid kit in a clearly marked, easily accessible location and inform your guests of its whereabouts.

Emergency Contacts and Information

Providing clear and concise emergency information is crucial. Create a guide with important phone numbers, including local emergency services, nearby hospitals, and your contact information. Post this guide in a visible spot, such as the kitchen or entryway, so guests can quickly find it in case of an emergency.

Secure Locks and Windows

Ensure that all doors and windows have secure locks. Guests need to feel safe and secure while staying in your home. Check that all locks are functioning correctly and consider installing deadbolts or additional security features on main entry points. Provide clear instructions on how to use the locks and any security systems you have in place.

Adequate Lighting

Good lighting is essential for safety. Ensure that all entryways, pathways, and common areas are well-lit. Motion-sensor lights can be particularly useful for outdoor areas, providing illumination when guests arrive at night. Inside, ensure that stairways and hallways are adequately lit to prevent trips and falls.

Childproofing

If you host families with young children, consider childproofing your home. Cover electrical outlets, secure loose cords, and install safety gates if you have stairs. Remove or secure any potentially hazardous items, such as cleaning supplies or sharp objects, that are within a child's reach.

Clear Exits and Evacuation Plan

Ensure that all exits are clearly marked and unobstructed. Guests should be able to easily identify and access exits in case of an emergency. Create an evacuation plan that includes routes and instructions for safely leaving the home. Post this plan in a prominent location, such as on the back of the main entry door.

Safe Appliances and Electrical Systems

Regularly inspect your appliances and electrical systems to ensure they are in good working order. Replace any faulty or damaged appliances, and avoid overloading electrical outlets. Provide instructions for safely operating any appliances, particularly if they are not intuitive to use.

Internet Security

Internet security is also a part of overall safety. Ensure that your Wi-Fi network is secure with a strong password. Inform guests about your internet usage policies and provide guidance on how to connect securely.

Ensuring that your Airbnb is equipped with these essential safety features can significantly enhance the overall experience for your guests. Safety is not just about compliance; it's about showing that you care for the well-being of those who stay in your home. This attention to detail fosters trust and can lead to positive reviews and repeat bookings.

Chapter 3: Must-Have Amenities for Hosts

Kitchen Essentials: From Coffee Makers to Cutlery

The kitchen is often the heart of a home, and this holds true for an Airbnb as well. Whether your guests plan to cook full meals or just enjoy a morning coffee, a well-equipped kitchen can significantly enhance their experience. Let's explore the kitchen essentials that will ensure your guests have everything they need for a comfortable and convenient stay.

Coffee Makers and Beverage Supplies

A good coffee maker is a must-have in any Airbnb kitchen. Many guests start their day with a cup of coffee, and having a reliable coffee maker can make their stay more pleasant. Consider providing both a traditional drip coffee maker and a single-serve machine like a Keurig to cater to different preferences. Ensure you stock a variety of coffee options, including regular and decaf, along with filters, sugar, and creamer.

Don't forget about tea drinkers. Provide an electric kettle and a selection of teas. Having hot chocolate and instant coffee on hand can also be a nice touch. These small additions can make guests feel more at home and taken care of.

Cooking Essentials

Even if guests don't plan to cook elaborate meals, having basic cooking essentials is important. Start with a good set of pots and pans, including a large saucepan, a medium-sized pot, and a frying pan. Non-stick options are convenient and easy to clean.

Utensils such as spatulas, wooden spoons, tongs, and a whisk are necessary for meal preparation. Include measuring cups and spoons, as well as a set of mixing bowls. A cutting board and a set of sharp knives are crucial for food prep, so ensure they are of good quality and kept sharp.

For baking enthusiasts, consider adding a few baking essentials like a baking sheet, a muffin tin, and a casserole dish. These items can be particularly appreciated by guests who enjoy cooking.

Dishware and Cutlery

Provide enough dishware and cutlery for the maximum number of guests your Airbnb can accommodate. This includes plates, bowls, and cups for every guest, as well as a few extras. Offering both casual and more formal dining options, like mugs for coffee and glasses for wine, can enhance the dining experience.

A complete set of cutlery, including forks, knives, spoons, and teaspoons, is essential. Ensure these items are durable and well-maintained. Additionally, having serving utensils like a large spoon, a slotted spoon, and a ladle can be very useful.

Small Appliances

Small appliances can make a big difference in the functionality of your kitchen. A toaster and a microwave are basics that guests will expect. A blender can be a nice addition for guests who like to make smoothies or soups.

Consider including a rice cooker or an Instant Pot, as these appliances can simplify meal preparation and appeal to guests who prefer cooking at home. A hand mixer or a stand mixer can also be appreciated by guests who enjoy baking.

Kitchen Gadgets

A few well-chosen kitchen gadgets can greatly enhance the utility of your kitchen. A can opener, a bottle opener, and a corkscrew are must-haves. A vegetable peeler, a cheese grater, and a colander are also essential for meal prep.

Include items like a salad spinner, kitchen shears, and a garlic press to cater to more specific cooking needs. These gadgets might not be used by every guest, but they show attention to detail and can make cooking more enjoyable for those who use them.

Cleaning Supplies

A clean kitchen is a pleasant kitchen. Ensure you provide ample cleaning supplies, including dish soap, sponges, and dish towels. A dishwasher is a great convenience, but if you don't have one, a dish rack for drying dishes is essential.

Trash bags, recycling bins, and clear instructions for waste disposal are important for maintaining cleanliness. Consider providing basic cleaning sprays and wipes so guests can clean up spills easily.

Pantry Basics

Stocking a few pantry basics can be very helpful for your guests. Items like salt, pepper, cooking oil, and basic spices can make a big difference for those preparing meals. Including non-perishable items such as pasta, rice, and canned goods can be an added convenience.

Providing a few breakfast essentials, like cereal, oatmeal, or bread, can also be a thoughtful touch. These items can make your guests' stay more comfortable, especially for those arriving late or without immediate access to a grocery store.

A well-equipped kitchen is an essential part of a successful Airbnb. By ensuring you have all the necessary appliances, utensils, and supplies, you can provide a comfortable and convenient experience for your guests. This attention to detail not only enhances their stay but also encourages positive reviews and repeat visits.

AIRBNB KITCHEN CHECKLIST

big heart hosting

THE BASICS

- coffee & tea makings
- knives & cutting board
- oven, stove, mitts, mats
- skillets for the stove
- pots for the stove
- strainer
- pans for the oven
- mixing bowls
- basic utensils
- cups and dishes
- silverware
- measuring cups
- refrigerator & freezer
- sink, drying rack, soap
- trash can
- recycling

GREAT ADDITIONS

- wine glasses & tumblers
- hand & paper towels
- salt & pepper
- olive oil and vinegar
- toaster
- microwave

BEST KEPT SECRETS

- welcome snack
- spices & baking gear
- clear counter space
- food storage
- garbage disposal
- dishwasher
- utensils 2.0

CLICK HERE TO READ THE FULL BLOG POST!

Kitchen Essentials. Source: bighearthosting.com.

Bedroom Comforts: Bedding, Pillows, and More

Creating a cozy and inviting bedroom is crucial for ensuring your guests have a restful stay. A comfortable bed with high-quality bedding, pillows, and thoughtful touches can make a significant difference in their experience. Let's explore how to make the bedroom in your Airbnb a haven of comfort and relaxation.

The Bed: Foundation of Comfort

The bed is the centerpiece of any bedroom, and it's where guests will spend a significant portion of their stay. Start with a good-quality mattress that offers support and comfort. Memory foam or hybrid mattresses are popular choices because they provide a balance of firmness and softness, catering to a wide range of preferences.

Ensure the bed frame is sturdy and doesn't creak or wobble. The stability of the bed contributes to a restful sleep, free from disturbances. Consider adding a mattress protector to keep the mattress clean and hygienic for each guest.

Bedding: Softness and Warmth

High-quality bedding is essential for a comfortable sleep. Invest in soft, breathable sheets made from materials like cotton or linen. These fabrics are gentle on the skin and regulate temperature well, keeping guests comfortable throughout the night.

Provide a duvet or comforter that is appropriate for the climate. In colder regions, a thicker, warmer duvet is ideal, while in warmer areas, a lighter comforter or quilt will suffice. Adding a blanket or throw at the foot of the bed gives guests an extra layer they can use if needed.

Choose a duvet cover and pillowcases that complement the room's decor. Neutral colors and simple patterns are versatile and appeal to most guests, while brighter colors and bold designs can add a touch of personality.

Pillows: Variety and Support

Pillows are a critical component of a comfortable bed. Offer a variety of pillows with different levels of firmness to cater to different sleeping preferences. Typically, providing two pillows per guest is a good rule of thumb.

Consider including both firm and soft pillows, as well as hypoallergenic options. Some guests may have allergies, and hypoallergenic pillows can enhance their comfort and health during their stay. Pillow protectors can also help keep pillows clean and fresh.

Additional Comforts: Beyond the Basics

Small touches can elevate the bedroom experience. Nightstands on either side of the bed provide a place for guests to keep personal items like phones, glasses, or books. Ensure there are lamps on each nightstand, offering guests a convenient lighting option for reading or relaxing before sleep.

A full-length mirror is a useful addition, allowing guests to get ready with ease. If space allows, a small dresser or chest of drawers can provide extra storage for clothing and personal items, making guests feel more at home.

Consider adding blackout curtains or blinds to ensure guests can sleep in darkness, even if they are sensitive to light. These can be particularly appreciated by guests who are adjusting to different time zones or who need to sleep during the day.

Personal Touches: Making It Special

Adding personal touches to the bedroom can make your guests feel welcome and valued. Fresh flowers in a vase, a selection of books or magazines, and a few decorative cushions can create a warm and inviting atmosphere. A welcome note with a few local tips or a small treat can also make a great impression.

Ensure there are enough outlets near the bed for guests to charge their devices. Providing a charging station or a few extra power strips can be very convenient for guests traveling with multiple devices.

Maintaining a high standard of cleanliness in the bedroom is crucial. Regularly wash all bedding, including pillowcases, duvet covers, and sheets, to ensure they are fresh for each new guest. Dust and vacuum the room thoroughly to maintain a clean and inviting space.

Creating a comfortable and well-equipped bedroom is an investment in your guests' satisfaction. When guests feel at home and well-rested, they are more likely to leave positive reviews and return for future stays. Your attention to detail and commitment to comfort will make your Airbnb stand out and ensure a memorable experience for all who stay.

Comfortable Airbnb Bedroom. Source: airbnb.com.

Bathroom Basics: Towels, Toiletries, and Beyond

A well-appointed bathroom is essential for making your Airbnb guests feel comfortable and pampered. The bathroom is a space where guests expect cleanliness, functionality, and a touch of luxury. Providing the right towels, toiletries, and additional amenities can transform an ordinary bathroom into a welcoming retreat. Here's how to ensure your bathroom meets and exceeds guest expectations.

Towels: Soft and Plentiful

Start with a good supply of high-quality towels. Soft, fluffy towels can make a big difference in your guests' experience. Provide at least two bath towels, one hand towel, and one washcloth per guest. Having extra towels on hand is also a good idea in case guests need more.

Ensure that the towels are absorbent and quick-drying. Cotton towels are a popular choice due to their softness and durability. Display the towels neatly, either on towel racks, shelves, or in a basket, to make them easily accessible.

Toiletries: Essential and Thoughtful

Providing essential toiletries is a simple way to show your guests that you care about their comfort. At a minimum, supply shampoo, conditioner, and body wash. Opt for products that are gentle on the skin and suitable for a variety of hair types. Consider using eco-friendly and refillable options to reduce waste and appeal to environmentally conscious guests.

In addition to these basics, offering extra amenities like lotion, facial cleanser, and toothpaste can be a pleasant surprise for your guests. Make sure all products are clearly labeled and replenished regularly.

Shower and Bath: Clean and Inviting

A clean and inviting shower or bath is crucial. Ensure the showerhead is in good working order and provides a strong, consistent flow of water. If you have a bathtub, make sure it is spotless and free from stains. Provide a non-slip mat in the shower or bath area to ensure safety.

Consider adding a shower caddy or shelf to keep toiletries organized and within easy reach. If space allows, a small stool or bench in the bathroom can provide a convenient place to sit or to store extra towels and toiletries.

Additional Comforts: Beyond the Basics

Small touches can elevate the bathroom experience for your guests. A soft bath mat outside the shower or bath adds comfort and prevents slipping. Ensure there is ample toilet paper and consider providing a few extra rolls in a visible location.

A hairdryer is a standard expectation for many travelers, so include one in the bathroom. Make sure it is easy to find and use. A magnifying mirror, cotton swabs, and cotton pads are thoughtful additions that guests will appreciate.

Keep the bathroom smelling fresh with a subtle air freshener or by using natural options like essential oil diffusers. Ensure that the bathroom is well-ventilated to prevent mold and mildew, and regularly check and clean any ventilation fans.

Storage and Organization: Practical and Neat

Adequate storage and organization are key to maintaining a tidy and functional bathroom. Provide hooks or racks for guests to hang their towels and robes. A small basket or tray for personal items like jewelry or watches can also be useful.

If your bathroom has cabinets or drawers, designate a few spaces for guest use and stock them with extra toiletries and essentials. Clear labeling can help guests feel comfortable using these items without hesitation.

A well-lit bathroom is essential. Make sure the lighting is bright enough for grooming tasks like shaving or applying makeup. If possible, include a combination of overhead lighting and task lighting around the mirror.

Maintaining cleanliness in the bathroom is paramount. Regularly clean all surfaces, including the sink, toilet, and shower or tub. Ensure that mirrors are spotless and that there is no residue or buildup on any fixtures. Fresh flowers or a small plant can add a touch of nature and freshness to the space.

By paying attention to these details, you can create a bathroom that is not only functional but also inviting and luxurious. When guests feel taken care of in every aspect, including their bathroom experience, they are more likely to enjoy their stay and leave positive reviews. Your commitment to comfort and cleanliness will shine through, making your Airbnb a preferred choice for travelers.

AIRBNB BATHROOM CHECKLIST

big heart hosting

THE BASICS

- plenty of toilet paper
- hand soap
- four soft towel sets
- wall or door hooks
- hot water
- shampoo & body wash
- floor mat
- lined trash can

GREAT ADDITIONS

- hand lotion
- conditioner
- mirror with good light
- surface for toiletries
- good ventilation
- hair dryer
- outlet with night light
- plunger

BEST KEPT SECRETS

- plumbing reminder
- air freshener
- reliable plumber
- tampons or pads
- first aid kit
- clothing drying rack
- backup soap
- travel size toiletries

CLICK HERE TO READ THE FULL BLOG POST!

Bathroom Essentials. Source: bighearthosting.com.

Chapter 4: Creating an Outstanding Guest Experience

Personal Touches: Adding Character to Your Space

One of the key elements that set Airbnb apart from traditional hotels is the unique and personal touch that hosts can bring to their space. These personal touches can make your guests feel more at home and create memorable experiences that they will cherish. Let's explore how you can add character to your space and make it stand out.

Reflecting Local Culture and Style

Incorporate elements that reflect the local culture and style of your area. This could be through artwork, textiles, or decorative items that showcase the region's heritage and traditions. For example, if your Airbnb is in a coastal town, consider using beach-inspired decor such as seashells, nautical art, or driftwood accents. In a city known for its vibrant art scene, display works by local artists or prints that celebrate the local culture.

Thoughtful Details and Decor

Pay attention to the small details that can enhance the overall ambiance of your space. Soft throw blankets, decorative cushions, and stylish rugs can add warmth and comfort. Choose colors and patterns that complement each other and create a cohesive look. Fresh flowers or potted plants can bring a touch of nature indoors and make the space feel more inviting.

Personal items such as books, magazines, and board games can make guests feel at home. Provide a selection of reading materials that cater to various interests, and consider including a few local guidebooks or maps to help guests explore the area.

Creating a Cozy Atmosphere

Lighting plays a crucial role in setting the mood of your space. Use a combination of ambient, task, and accent lighting to create a cozy and welcoming atmosphere. Soft, warm lighting in the living and bedroom areas can make the space feel more inviting, while brighter task lighting in the kitchen and bathroom ensures functionality.

Consider adding candles or fairy lights for an extra touch of warmth and charm. These can be especially appreciated by guests looking to relax in the evening or create a romantic setting.

Personal Greetings and Welcome Gifts

A personal greeting or welcome gift can make a big impact on your guests. A handwritten note expressing your excitement to host them and providing a few local tips can make guests feel special. Welcome gifts such as a bottle of wine, local snacks, or a small souvenir can create a lasting impression.

If you have the opportunity to meet your guests in person, a warm greeting and a quick tour of the space can make them feel more comfortable and help establish a positive relationship. However, if an in-person meeting is not possible, clear and friendly communication through messages can also achieve this.

Functional and Aesthetic Balance

While it's important to add character and charm, remember to strike a balance between aesthetics and functionality. Ensure that all decorative items serve a purpose and do not clutter the space. Guests should feel that the decor enhances their stay without being overwhelming or impractical.

For example, a beautiful but comfortable armchair can serve both as a decorative piece and a cozy spot for guests to relax. Similarly, attractive storage solutions like stylish baskets or shelving units can keep the space organized and add to the decor.

Personalizing the Experience

Consider the needs and preferences of your typical guests and tailor your space to meet those expectations. For instance, if you often host families, include toys, games, or children's books. For business travelers, provide a comfortable workspace with necessary supplies like a desk lamp and charging stations.

Personal touches that cater to specific guest needs can greatly enhance their experience and show that you care about their comfort and enjoyment.

Adding character to your Airbnb is all about creating a space that feels warm, inviting, and uniquely yours. By incorporating local elements, thoughtful details, and a balance of functionality and aesthetics, you can provide a memorable and personalized experience for your guests. These personal touches not only make your space stand out but also contribute to the overall charm and appeal that keep guests coming back.

Example of Small Personal Touche. Source: amazon.com.

Technology and Connectivity: Wi-Fi, Smart TVs, and More

In today's digital age, providing reliable technology and connectivity is essential for a successful Airbnb experience. Guests expect to stay connected, entertained, and productive during their stay. Ensuring your space is equipped with modern technology can significantly enhance their experience. Let's explore how to meet and exceed these expectations.

Reliable Wi-Fi: The Backbone of Connectivity

Wi-Fi is one of the most important amenities for any Airbnb. Whether guests need to work remotely, stream movies, or stay in touch with family, a reliable internet connection is crucial. Invest in a high-speed internet plan that can handle multiple devices simultaneously. Ensure that the Wi-Fi signal is strong throughout your property, including all bedrooms and living areas.

Clearly display the Wi-Fi network name and password in an easy-to-find location, such as in your welcome guide or on a card in the living room. If possible, provide a backup internet option, such as a mobile hotspot, in case of temporary outages.

Smart TVs: Entertainment at Their Fingertips

Smart TVs are a great addition to your Airbnb, offering guests access to a wide range of entertainment options. With a smart TV, guests can stream their favorite shows and movies from platforms like Netflix, Hulu, and Amazon Prime. Ensure that the TV is easy to use and that streaming apps are set up and ready to go.

Provide clear instructions on how to operate the TV and any connected devices. Consider including a small selection of local channels or a digital antenna for guests who prefer traditional TV viewing. If your guests are likely to bring their own devices, ensure there are HDMI cables or other necessary connectors available.

Charging Stations: Keeping Devices Powered

Guests often travel with multiple devices, including smartphones, tablets, and laptops. Providing convenient charging options can enhance their stay. Place charging stations or power strips with multiple outlets and USB ports in key areas, such as beside the bed and in the living room.

Make sure there are enough outlets for all guests to charge their devices simultaneously. Consider labeling the charging stations for ease of use and providing a variety of charging cables to accommodate different device types.

Home Automation: Enhancing Comfort and Convenience

Home automation can add an extra layer of comfort and convenience for your guests. Smart thermostats allow guests to easily control the temperature to their liking, ensuring a comfortable environment. Smart lighting systems can provide customizable lighting options, creating the perfect ambiance for any occasion.

Voice-activated assistants, like Amazon Alexa or Google Home, can offer guests hands-free control over various aspects of the home, from playing music to providing local information. Ensure these devices are set up and provide clear instructions on how to use them.

Security and Privacy: Peace of Mind

Technology can also enhance the security and privacy of your Airbnb. Install smart locks that allow for keyless entry, making it easy for guests to check in and out without needing to exchange physical keys. Ensure that the entry code is unique for each guest and change it between stays.

Security cameras on the exterior of your property can provide an added sense of security, but be sure to respect guests' privacy by not installing cameras inside the home. Clearly inform guests of any security measures in place and how they work.

Sound Systems: Enhancing the Atmosphere

A good sound system can enhance the ambiance of your Airbnb. Consider providing a Bluetooth speaker or a soundbar that guests can easily connect to their devices. This allows them to enjoy their favorite music or podcasts during their stay.

Place the sound system in a central location and provide simple instructions for use. If possible, offer a selection of playlists or recommend local radio stations to help guests feel more at home.

Work-Friendly Features: Supporting Remote Work

With the rise of remote work, many guests may need a functional workspace during their stay. Provide a dedicated area with a comfortable desk and chair, good lighting, and easy access to power outlets. Ensure the Wi-Fi signal is strong in this area and consider providing basic office supplies like pens, paper, and a printer.

A well-equipped workspace can attract business travelers and remote workers, increasing the appeal of your Airbnb.

Incorporating modern technology and connectivity into your Airbnb is essential for meeting the needs of today's travelers. By providing reliable Wi-Fi, smart TVs, convenient charging stations, home automation, security features, sound systems, and work-friendly spaces, you can ensure a comfortable and enjoyable stay for your guests. These technological amenities not only enhance the guest experience but also set your property apart in a competitive market.

Local Guides and Recommendations: Helping Guests Explore

One of the joys of staying at an Airbnb is experiencing a new place through the eyes of a local. As a host, you have the unique opportunity to provide guests with insights and recommendations that can make their visit truly special. Here's how you can help your guests explore and enjoy the local area.

Curating Local Guides

Creating a comprehensive local guide is a wonderful way to introduce guests to the best your area has to offer. Start with an overview of the neighborhood, highlighting key attractions, popular restaurants, and essential services like grocery stores and pharmacies. Include a map with marked locations to make it easy for guests to navigate.

Consider creating themed guides based on different interests. For example, a foodie guide could highlight the best local eateries, from breakfast spots to fine dining restaurants. An outdoor adventure guide might focus on nearby parks, hiking trails, and recreational activities. Tailoring your guides to various interests can cater to a wider range of guests and enhance their experience.

Personal Recommendations

Personal recommendations add a special touch to your local guide. Share your favorite spots that might not be well-known to tourists but are beloved by locals. This could include a cozy café with the best coffee, a hidden gem of a bookstore, or a scenic lookout point for sunset views.

Describe why you love these places and what makes them special. Personal anecdotes and stories can make your recommendations more engaging and relatable. Guests will appreciate the insider knowledge and feel more connected to the community.

Dining and Nightlife

Guests often look forward to exploring the local dining and nightlife scene. Provide a variety of dining options, ranging from casual eateries to upscale restaurants. Include a mix of cuisines to cater to different tastes and dietary preferences. Mention any standout dishes or specialties that guests should try.

For nightlife, recommend local bars, clubs, and live music venues. Highlight places with unique atmospheres, signature cocktails, or notable events. Ensure to mention any age restrictions or dress codes if applicable.

Attractions and Activities

Guide your guests to must-see attractions and activities in the area. Include major tourist sites as well as off-the-beaten-path destinations. Describe what each place offers, its significance, and any tips for visiting, such as the best times to go or how to avoid crowds.

Suggest activities that showcase the local culture and heritage. This could be visiting museums, attending cultural festivals, or exploring historical landmarks. Encourage guests to participate in local experiences that provide a deeper understanding of the area.

Practical Information

In addition to fun and leisure, provide practical information that can help guests during their stay. List essential services such as nearby hospitals, pharmacies, and convenience stores. Include emergency contact numbers and addresses for urgent needs.

Detail transportation options, including public transit routes, taxi services, and car rental locations. Providing information on parking regulations and tips for navigating the area can also be very helpful, especially for guests unfamiliar with the region.

Interactive Experiences

Encourage guests to immerse themselves in the local culture through interactive experiences. Suggest local tours, cooking classes, or craft workshops that allow them to engage with the community. Highlight any seasonal events or markets that might be happening during their stay.

If possible, arrange partnerships with local businesses to offer discounts or exclusive experiences for your guests. This not only enhances their stay but also supports local enterprises.

Digital and Print Formats

Offer your local guides and recommendations in both digital and print formats. A digital guide can be easily accessed on a smartphone or tablet, while a printed version can be a thoughtful touch left in the rental for guests to browse at their leisure. Ensure the information is up-to-date and refresh it regularly to reflect any changes in the local scene.

By providing detailed and personalized local guides, you help guests make the most of their visit and create memorable experiences. Your insights and recommendations can transform their stay, making it not just a visit but a genuine exploration of what makes your area unique and special. This thoughtful gesture not only enhances their overall experience but also fosters a deeper connection to the place and the community.

Host Recommendations for Guests. Source: etsy.com.

Chapter 5:
Communication and Guest Interaction

Before Arrival: Setting Clear Expectations

Setting clear expectations before your guests arrive is crucial for ensuring a smooth and enjoyable stay. Effective communication can prevent misunderstandings and help guests feel confident and prepared. Here's how to establish these expectations clearly and warmly.

Communicating House Rules

Start by clearly communicating your house rules. These guidelines help guests understand what is expected of them during their stay. Cover important topics such as smoking policies, pet policies, noise levels, and any restrictions on parties or events. Be clear but friendly in your tone, emphasizing that these rules are in place to ensure a comfortable experience for everyone.

For example, if you have a no-smoking policy, you might say, "We kindly ask that you refrain from smoking inside the house to keep the space fresh for all guests." This approach is polite and explains the reason behind the rule.

Check-In and Check-Out Procedures

Providing detailed information about check-in and check-out procedures can help guests plan their arrival and departure smoothly. Specify the check-in and check-out times, and outline the steps they need to follow. If you use a keyless entry system, provide clear instructions on how to use it. If you will be meeting guests in person, let them know where and when to meet you.

For instance, you might write, "Check-in is from 3 PM onwards. You can access the property using the keyless entry code provided in this message. If you need any assistance, I will be available to help."

Directions and Parking

Give detailed directions to your property to ensure guests can find it easily. Include landmarks, street names, and any other helpful details. If your property is in a complex or gated community, provide instructions on how to navigate those areas.

Include information about parking. Let guests know where they can park and any relevant rules, such as permit requirements or designated spots. For example, "There is free street parking available directly in front of the house. Please avoid parking in the neighbor's driveway."

Amenities and Supplies

Inform guests about the amenities and supplies available in your Airbnb. Highlight features such as Wi-Fi, kitchen appliances, laundry facilities, and entertainment options. Providing this information beforehand helps guests pack appropriately and reduces inquiries during their stay.

You might say, "Our home is equipped with high-speed Wi-Fi, a fully stocked kitchen, and a washer and dryer for your convenience. Towels, linens, and basic toiletries are also provided."

Emergency Information

Sharing emergency information is essential for guest safety. Provide the location of the nearest hospital, pharmacy, and emergency contact numbers. Include instructions on how to use safety equipment, such as fire extinguishers or first aid kits.

For example, "In case of an emergency, the nearest hospital is St. Mary's, located at 123 Main Street. A first aid kit is located under the bathroom sink, and the fire extinguisher is in the kitchen pantry."

Local Recommendations

To enhance your guests' experience, share some local recommendations before they arrive. Suggest nearby restaurants, cafes, attractions, and activities. This gesture shows that you care about their stay and want them to enjoy the area.

You might include, "For a great breakfast, visit Joe's Café just a few blocks away. Don't miss the scenic walking trail at Riverside Park, perfect for a morning stroll."

Personal Welcome Message

A warm, personal welcome message can make guests feel valued and excited about their stay. Introduce yourself briefly and express your enthusiasm for hosting them. This message sets a positive tone and opens the line of communication.

For example, "Hi [Guest's Name], I'm [Your Name], and I'm thrilled to host you! Please feel free to reach out if you have any questions or need recommendations. I hope you have a fantastic stay!"

By setting clear expectations before arrival, you help guests feel prepared and welcomed. This proactive communication can significantly enhance their experience, making their stay smooth, enjoyable, and memorable.

Dear Guest,

Welcome! We're so happy you arrived safely and hope you had no troubles in your travels here!
We want you to consider this house your home away from home , even if you're only here a few days. If you have any questions, you can reach out to us by cell at xxx-xxx-xxxx or through email at xx@xxx.com

We hope you have a wonderful stay !

sincerely , brooke and Thomas

Welcome Message Example. Source: postermywall.com.

During the Stay: Being Available and Responsive

Being available and responsive during your guests' stay is key to ensuring they have a positive experience. This involves maintaining open lines of communication, addressing issues promptly, and providing assistance as needed. Here's how you can be an attentive and supportive host.

Open Communication Channels

Establish clear communication channels from the beginning. Let your guests know the best way to reach you, whether it's through the Airbnb messaging system, text, or phone. Make it clear that you are available for any questions or concerns they might have during their stay.

For example, you might write, "Feel free to contact me via Airbnb messages if you need anything or have any questions. I usually respond within an hour."

Welcoming Check-In

When guests first arrive, a welcoming check-in can set a positive tone. If you're meeting them in person, greet them warmly and offer a quick tour of the property. Point out essential features and any amenities they might need. If you're using self-check-in, send a friendly message to ensure they have arrived safely and have everything they need.

You might say, "I hope you've settled in comfortably! Please let me know if you need any assistance or have any questions about the house or the area."

Prompt Issue Resolution

No matter how well-prepared your property is, issues can sometimes arise. The key is to address them promptly and effectively. Whether it's a minor inconvenience like a missing kitchen utensil or a larger issue like a plumbing problem, show your guests that you are committed to resolving it quickly.

For instance, if a guest reports a leaky faucet, respond with, "I'm sorry to hear about the faucet. I will have a plumber come over as soon as possible to fix it. Thank you for bringing it to my attention."

Providing Local Assistance

Your local knowledge is a valuable resource for your guests. Be ready to provide recommendations for dining, entertainment, and transportation. If guests encounter any difficulties navigating the area, such as finding a local store or understanding public transit, offer your assistance.

For example, "If you're looking for a great place to eat, I highly recommend La Bella Pizzeria just down the street. They have fantastic pasta and pizza."

Checking In Without Intruding

While it's important to be available, it's equally important to respect your guests' privacy. A friendly check-in message once during their stay can show that you care without being intrusive. This can be a simple message asking if everything is going well and if they need anything.

You could say, "Hi there! I hope you're enjoying your stay. Just wanted to check in to see if everything is going well. Let me know if there's anything you need!"

Providing Essential Information

Ensure that your guests have all the information they need to make the most of their stay. This includes Wi-Fi passwords, appliance instructions, and guidelines for using amenities. Make sure this information is easily accessible, either in a welcome booklet or a digital guide.

For instance, "The Wi-Fi network is 'HomeSweetHome' and the password is 'Welcome123'. You'll find a manual for the coffee maker in the kitchen drawer."

Handling Emergencies

In case of emergencies, be prepared to act quickly and efficiently. Provide clear instructions on what to do in case of fire, medical emergencies, or other urgent situations. Make sure guests know where to find emergency contacts and equipment like fire extinguishers and first aid kits.

For example, "In case of emergency, dial 911. The fire extinguisher is located under the kitchen sink, and the first aid kit is in the bathroom cabinet."

Departure and Farewell

As the end of your guests' stay approaches, make sure they are clear on the check-out process. Provide instructions on what to do with keys, how to leave the property, and any final steps they need to take. A friendly farewell message can leave a lasting positive impression.

You might say, "I hope you've had a wonderful stay! Check-out time is 11 AM. Please leave the keys on the kitchen table. Safe travels, and I hope to host you again in the future!"

Being available and responsive during your guests' stay helps create a supportive and enjoyable environment. By maintaining clear communication, addressing issues promptly, and offering assistance when needed, you can ensure that your guests feel well cared for and have a memorable stay.

After Checkout: Gathering Feedback and Reviews

Once your guests have checked out, your interaction with them is not quite over. Gathering feedback and encouraging reviews is a crucial part of improving your Airbnb and maintaining high standards. This process helps you understand what you did well and what can be improved, ensuring future guests have an even better experience. Here's how to effectively gather feedback and reviews.

Prompt and Polite Follow-Up

Shortly after your guests check out, send a friendly message thanking them for their stay and inviting them to leave feedback. Timing is important; contacting them within 24 hours of their departure keeps their experience fresh in their minds.

You might write, "Thank you for staying at our place! I hope you had a great time. If you have a moment, I'd appreciate it if you could leave a review about your experience. Your feedback helps us improve and continue to provide a great experience for future guests."

Encouraging Honest Reviews

Encouraging guests to leave honest reviews is key to getting valuable insights. Let them know that their genuine feedback is important and that you welcome both positive comments and constructive criticism.

For example, "We value your honest feedback and would love to hear about what you enjoyed and what we could improve. Your input helps us enhance the stay for future guests."

Making It Easy

Make the review process as easy as possible for your guests. Provide clear instructions on how to leave a review on the Airbnb platform. If there were specific aspects of their stay that you'd like feedback on, feel free to ask about those directly, but keep the request simple and straightforward.

You could say, "To leave a review, simply log into your Airbnb account, go to your reservations, and click on 'Leave a Review' for your recent stay. Any comments about the cleanliness, amenities, or your overall experience would be greatly appreciated."

Responding to Reviews

Responding to reviews shows that you value guest feedback and are committed to continuous improvement. Thank guests for positive reviews and address any concerns mentioned in less favorable ones. This demonstrates your dedication to providing an excellent guest experience and can enhance your reputation on the platform.

For a positive review, you might respond, "Thank you for your kind words! We're thrilled you enjoyed your stay and hope to welcome you back in the future."

If a guest raises an issue, acknowledge it and explain any steps you're taking to address it. For instance, "Thank you for your feedback. We're sorry to hear about the noise issue and are working on better soundproofing the space to ensure a quieter stay for future guests."

Using Feedback to Improve

Take the feedback you receive seriously and use it to make tangible improvements to your Airbnb. If multiple guests mention a particular issue, prioritize addressing it. Whether it's adding more kitchen supplies, improving the Wi-Fi, or enhancing cleanliness, acting on feedback shows that you're attentive and committed to providing the best possible experience.

For example, if guests frequently mention that the check-in process was confusing, consider updating your instructions or adding more signage to help guests find their way.

Keeping Communication Open

Encourage guests to reach out with any further comments or questions even after they've left their review. Maintaining an open line of communication can foster long-term relationships and potentially turn one-time visitors into repeat guests.

You could say, "If you have any additional feedback or questions, please don't hesitate to contact me. We'd love to host you again in the future!"

Continuous Engagement

Stay engaged with past guests by sending occasional updates or special offers. This can keep your Airbnb top of mind for their future travel plans and encourage repeat bookings.

For instance, "We're excited to announce a new feature in our home: a cozy outdoor fire pit perfect for evening gatherings. We'd love to host you again soon!"

Gathering feedback and reviews after checkout is essential for understanding and improving the guest experience. By following up promptly, encouraging honest reviews, making the process easy, and using the feedback to make improvements, you can continually enhance your Airbnb and ensure high guest satisfaction.

Chapter 6: Pricing and Policies

Setting Competitive Prices: Factors to Consider

Determining the right price for your Airbnb is crucial to attracting guests while ensuring you meet your financial goals. Setting competitive prices involves understanding several key factors that influence what guests are willing to pay. Here's a guide to help you set prices that balance attractiveness and profitability.

Analyzing the Market

Start by researching the local market. Look at other Airbnb listings in your area that are similar to your property in terms of size, amenities, and location. Note their pricing strategies, including nightly rates, cleaning fees, and any additional charges. Pay attention to their occupancy rates and guest reviews, as these can provide insights into how well their pricing is working.

Understanding your competition helps you position your property effectively. If you're new to hosting, consider pricing slightly below similar listings to attract your first few guests and build up positive reviews.

Considering Seasonality

Seasonality plays a significant role in pricing. Demand for Airbnb rentals can vary greatly depending on the time of year. Identify peak seasons, such as holidays, local events, and popular vacation periods, when demand is higher. During these times, you can increase your rates to maximize revenue.

Conversely, during off-peak seasons, consider lowering your prices to attract more bookings. Offering discounts for longer stays or last-minute bookings during slow periods can also help maintain a steady occupancy rate.

Evaluating Your Property's Unique Features

Highlighting and pricing based on your property's unique features can give you a competitive edge. If your Airbnb offers special amenities such as a hot tub, stunning views, proximity to major attractions, or a unique design, factor these into your pricing strategy. Guests are often willing to pay more for properties that offer something extra or cater to specific needs.

For example, a centrally located apartment with modern amenities can command higher prices compared to properties in less desirable areas or with fewer features.

Understanding Guest Demographics

Consider the types of guests your property attracts. Are they business travelers, families, couples, or solo adventurers? Each group has different needs and budget constraints. Business travelers might prioritize location and convenience and be willing to pay a premium for it, while families might look for value and space.

Tailor your pricing to suit the needs and expectations of your target audience. Offering packages or additional services, such as guided tours or airport transfers, can also appeal to specific guest segments and justify higher rates.

Utilizing Dynamic Pricing Tools

Dynamic pricing tools can help you adjust your rates in real-time based on various factors, including demand, competition, and market trends. These tools analyze data to recommend optimal pricing, helping you stay competitive without constant manual adjustments.

Platforms like Airbnb often have built-in pricing tools that suggest rates based on similar listings in your area. Using these tools can save time and ensure your prices remain competitive.

Calculating Costs and Desired Profit

Ensure that your pricing covers all expenses related to hosting, including mortgage or rent, utilities, cleaning services, supplies, maintenance, and platform fees. Calculate a base rate that covers these costs and then add a margin for profit.

It's important to strike a balance between covering your costs and setting a price that attracts guests. Overpricing can deter potential guests, while underpricing can lead to losses.

Setting a Minimum and Maximum Price

Establishing a minimum price ensures you cover your basic costs, even during low-demand periods. Setting a maximum price for peak times or special events helps you capitalize on high demand without appearing exorbitant.

Review and adjust these limits regularly based on your occupancy rates and feedback from guests. Flexibility and responsiveness to market conditions are key to maintaining optimal pricing.

Gathering and Using Feedback

After hosting several guests, gather feedback about your pricing. Pay attention to any comments regarding value for money. If guests consistently mention that your property is a great deal or suggest improvements that could justify higher rates, use this information to adjust your pricing strategy.

Regularly reviewing your pricing based on feedback and market trends ensures you remain competitive and attractive to potential guests.

Setting competitive prices for your Airbnb involves a careful analysis of the market, understanding seasonality, leveraging unique property features, and utilizing dynamic pricing tools. By considering these factors, you can set prices that attract guests while ensuring your financial goals are met.

Creating House Rules: Clear and Fair Policies

Establishing clear and fair house rules is essential for maintaining a smooth and enjoyable experience for both hosts and guests. Well-defined rules set expectations, help prevent misunderstandings, and ensure that everyone is on the same page regarding behavior and responsibilities. Here's how to create house rules that are both effective and easy to understand.

Defining Your Non-Negotiables

Start by identifying the non-negotiable rules that are crucial for maintaining your property and ensuring the safety and comfort of your guests. These might include rules about smoking, pets, noise levels, and the maximum number of guests allowed. Be specific and clear in your wording to avoid any ambiguity.

For example, instead of saying "No smoking," specify "Smoking is not allowed inside the house. Guests may smoke on the patio, but please dispose of cigarette butts responsibly."

Addressing Common Issues

Think about common issues that might arise during a guest's stay and create rules to address them. These can include guidelines on parking, trash disposal, use of appliances, and quiet hours. Clear instructions help guests navigate these situations without confusion.

For instance, "Please park only in the designated parking spot in front of the house. Additional parking is available on the street if needed."

Being Respectful and Polite

The tone of your house rules should be respectful and polite. You want to communicate the importance of these rules without sounding overly strict or unwelcoming. Use positive language and explain the reason behind each rule when necessary, as this helps guests understand and appreciate your perspective.

For example, "To ensure a pleasant experience for all our neighbors, please keep noise levels down after 10 PM. Thank you for your understanding and cooperation."

Including Safety Guidelines

Safety guidelines are a crucial part of house rules. Inform guests about the location and use of safety equipment like fire extinguishers and first aid kits. Provide instructions for emergencies and clarify any safety protocols specific to your property.

For example, "In case of a fire, please use the fire extinguisher located under the kitchen sink. For medical emergencies, a first aid kit is available in the bathroom cabinet."

Being Flexible When Possible

While some rules are non-negotiable, try to be flexible where possible to enhance the guest experience. Consider allowing exceptions under certain conditions or providing alternatives that meet both your needs and those of your guests.

For example, if you generally don't allow pets but can make an exception for small, well-behaved animals, state this clearly: "We usually do not allow pets, but small, well-behaved pets may be considered upon request. Please contact us to discuss."

Encouraging Respect for Property and Neighbors

Encourage guests to treat your property and neighbors with respect. This includes guidelines on how to use appliances and furnishings, as well as expectations for cleanliness and consideration of shared spaces.

For instance, "Please use coasters on the wooden tables to prevent damage. We appreciate your help in keeping the house in great condition for future guests."

Providing Clear Check-In and Check-Out Instructions

Ensure your house rules include detailed check-in and check-out instructions. This helps guests plan their arrival and departure and ensures a smooth transition between bookings.

For example, "Check-in is from 3 PM onwards. Please use the keyless entry code provided. Check-out is by 11 AM. Before leaving, kindly ensure all windows are closed, and the front door is locked."

Communicating Rules Effectively

Once you have established your house rules, communicate them effectively to your guests. Include the rules in your Airbnb listing, and provide a printed copy in a welcome book or a visible location in the property. Remind guests of key rules during the booking process and upon arrival to ensure they are well-informed.

For example, "A full list of house rules can be found in the welcome book on the coffee table. Please take a moment to read through them upon arrival."

Creating clear and fair house rules is an essential part of hosting on Airbnb. By defining non-negotiables, addressing common issues, and communicating respectfully, you set the stage for a positive and enjoyable experience for both you and your guests.

Welcome

Name of your property

WIFI
NETWORK: 1234
PASSWORD: 1234

CONTACT

Host: Any Name
Phone: +000 123 456
Email: any@mail.com

EMERGENCY

Hospital
123 Avenue
tel: +000 123 456

Police
123 Avenue
tel: +000 123 456

CHECK OUT

Check-out: 11am
Please take the trash out before you leave.

HOUSE RULES

- No smoking allowed.
- No parties or events allowed.
- No pets allowed.
- No unregistered guests allowed.
- Please don't eat or drink in the bedrooms.
- Please respect the quiet hours from 11.00 pm to 7.00 am.
- Please turn off the AC when you go out.
- Please respect check-in and check-out hours.
- Please take care of the furnishings.
- You have to pay for damages that exceed the security deposit.
- No illegal substances allowed on the premises.

Handling Deposits and Damages: Protecting Your Property

Protecting your property from potential damages is a crucial aspect of being an Airbnb host. Handling damages efficiently and fairly can ensure your property remains in excellent condition while maintaining a good relationship with your guests. Here's how to manage this process effectively, given the restrictions on charging security deposits outside the Airbnb platform.

Understanding Airbnb's Security Deposit Policy

Airbnb does not allow hosts to charge a security deposit through their Resolution Center or outside the platform. Instead, guests are informed at the time of booking that their payment method may be charged for any damages incurred during their stay. This policy streamlines the process and provides clarity for both hosts and guests.

Communicating Your Policy

Clearly communicate your policy regarding damages to your guests before they book. Emphasize that while you do not charge a security deposit upfront, any damages will be charged to their payment method on file. Transparency helps prevent misunderstandings and ensures guests are aware of their responsibilities.

For example, in your listing description, you could state, "Please note that while we do not require a security deposit, any damages caused during your stay will be charged to your payment method on file with Airbnb."

Inspecting the Property

Before guests arrive, conduct a thorough inspection of your property. Document the condition of each room with photos or videos, focusing on valuable items and areas prone to wear and tear. This documentation serves as a reference point should any disputes arise after the guest's stay.

Repeat the inspection after the guests check out. Compare the property's condition with your initial documentation to identify any damages or missing items.

Reporting and Documenting Damages

If you discover any damages after a guest's stay, document them immediately. Take clear photos or videos and provide detailed descriptions of the damages. This documentation is crucial when filing a claim with Airbnb or discussing the issue with your guests.

For example, if a lamp is broken, take close-up photos of the damage and note the condition of the lamp before the guest's stay based on your initial inspection photos.

Filing a Claim with Airbnb

If you need to seek compensation for damages, file a claim through Airbnb's Resolution Center. Provide all relevant documentation, including photos, videos, and any receipts for repairs or replacements. Airbnb will review the evidence and mediate the dispute if necessary.

Ensure your claim is filed promptly, as delays can complicate the resolution process. Airbnb typically requires claims to be filed within 14 days of the guest's checkout or before the next guest checks in, whichever comes first.

Communicating with Guests

When addressing damages, communicate with your guests respectfully and clearly. Inform them of the damages you discovered and provide evidence. Explain the costs involved and that Airbnb will charge their payment method on file. This transparency helps maintain trust and can lead to a more amicable resolution.

For example, send a message like, "Dear [Guest's Name], I hope you enjoyed your stay. Unfortunately, I noticed a broken lamp in the living room after your departure. I've attached photos for your reference. The replacement cost is $50, which will be processed through Airbnb. Thank you for your understanding."

Preventative Measures

Taking preventative measures can minimize the risk of damages. Provide clear instructions on how to use appliances and any delicate items. Place protective covers on furniture and use durable materials for high-traffic areas. Regular maintenance and prompt repairs can also prevent minor issues from escalating into significant problems.

For instance, providing a guide on how to use the washing machine or placing coasters on all tables can help guests take better care of your property.

Offering Insurance Options

Consider purchasing short-term rental insurance to cover damages that exceed Airbnb's coverage or are not covered by their Host Guarantee. This additional layer of protection can give you peace of mind and financial security in case of significant damages or liability issues.

Many insurance companies offer policies tailored for Airbnb hosts, covering a range of incidents from property damage to personal liability.

Handling damages effectively involves clear communication, thorough documentation, respectful interaction with guests, and preventative measures. These steps ensure your property is well-protected while providing a positive experience for your guests.

Chapter 7: Marketing Your Listing

Taking Stunning Photos: First Impressions Matter

In the world of Airbnb, first impressions are crucial, and nothing makes a stronger initial impact than high-quality photos. Stunning photos can capture the essence of your property, highlight its best features, and entice potential guests to book. Here's how to take photos that make your listing stand out.

Preparing Your Space

Before you even pick up the camera, ensure your space is spotless and well-organized. Clean every room thoroughly, remove clutter, and arrange furniture neatly. Small touches like fresh flowers, neatly arranged cushions, and a welcoming setup can make a big difference.

Lighting is key to good photography. Shoot during the day when natural light is abundant. Open curtains and blinds to let in as much light as possible. Turn on all the lights in the room to enhance brightness, but avoid harsh overhead lights that can create unflattering shadows.

Choosing the Right Equipment

While professional photographers have specialized equipment, you can still achieve great results with a good smartphone or a basic digital camera. The key is to understand the capabilities of your device and use it effectively.

A tripod can be a valuable tool, helping you achieve steady shots and allowing you to experiment with different angles without the risk of blurry images. If you're using a smartphone, consider using a wide-angle lens attachment to capture more of the room in a single shot.

Capturing the Best Angles

The angle from which you take a photo can dramatically affect its appeal. Shoot from chest height to provide a natural perspective. Avoid extreme angles that can distort the room's dimensions. Taking photos from the corners of a room can often give a more comprehensive view and make the space appear larger.

Experiment with different angles to see which ones best capture the room's features. For example, photographing a living room from the doorway can provide a welcoming perspective, while a shot from a corner might showcase the space more fully.

Highlighting Key Features

Focus on what makes your property unique. If you have a beautiful fireplace, a stunning view, or a cozy reading nook, make sure to highlight these features. Take close-up shots that capture the details and ambiance of these areas.

Each room should be showcased with multiple photos, providing an overview as well as detailed shots of notable features. For instance, in the kitchen, include a wide shot of the entire space along with close-ups of high-end appliances or a beautifully set dining table.

Creating a Narrative

Your photos should tell a story about what it's like to stay at your property. Start with an inviting exterior shot, then guide viewers through the interior, room by room. This narrative approach helps potential guests visualize their stay and imagine themselves in the space.

Include shots of all key areas: living room, bedrooms, kitchen, bathrooms, and any outdoor spaces. Make sure to capture a variety of perspectives within each room to give a comprehensive sense of the layout and flow.

Editing for Perfection

Editing can enhance the quality of your photos, making them more appealing without misrepresenting the space. Basic adjustments to brightness, contrast, and saturation can make your images pop. Crop out any distracting elements and straighten lines to ensure a polished look.

Avoid over-editing, which can make photos look unnatural. The goal is to present your property in the best possible light while maintaining an honest representation.

Professional Assistance

If photography isn't your strong suit, consider hiring a professional photographer. The investment can pay off significantly in the form of increased bookings. Professionals have the expertise and equipment to capture your property at its best and can provide high-quality images that make a lasting impression.

Taking stunning photos for your Airbnb listing involves preparation, the right equipment, careful composition, and thoughtful editing. These efforts ensure that your listing stands out and attracts potential guests by showcasing your property in its best light. First impressions matter, and with great photos, you can make sure they are always positive.

 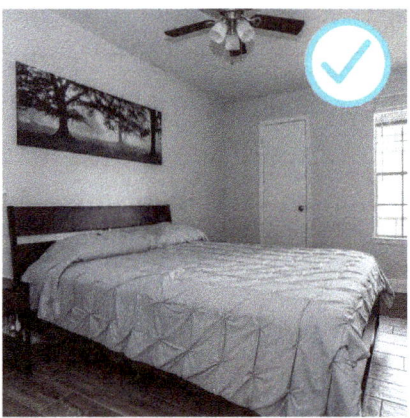

Example of High-Quality Photos. Source: missafir.com.

Writing an Engaging Description: Highlighting Key Features

An engaging description is crucial for attracting potential guests to your Airbnb listing. It should provide a clear, inviting, and honest portrayal of your property, highlighting its key features and unique qualities. Here's how to craft a description that captivates and informs.

Start with a Catchy Opening

Your opening sentence sets the tone for the entire description. It should grab attention and entice readers to learn more. Think about what makes your property special and lead with that.

For example, "Experience modern comfort in the heart of downtown, just steps away from the city's vibrant nightlife and cultural landmarks."

Highlight Key Features

Focus on the standout features that make your property unique. Describe amenities and elements that will appeal to potential guests. Use descriptive language that paints a vivid picture, but stay honest to avoid creating false expectations.

For instance, if your property has a beautiful view, you might say, "Wake up to breathtaking panoramic views of the city skyline from the comfort of your private balcony."

Describe Each Room

Give a brief overview of each room, highlighting its key features and amenities. Make sure to include details about the size, style, and any special touches that enhance the guest experience.

For the living room, you could write, "Relax in the spacious living room, featuring a plush sofa, a 50-inch smart TV, and large windows that flood the space with natural light."

For the kitchen, "Cook up a storm in the fully-equipped kitchen, complete with modern appliances, granite countertops, and all the cookware you'll need."

Mention Practical Details

While you want your description to be engaging, it's also important to include practical details that guests need to know. This includes the number of bedrooms and bathrooms, sleeping arrangements, and any special considerations like accessibility features.

For example, "This two-bedroom apartment offers one queen-sized bed in the master bedroom and two twin beds in the second bedroom, perfect for families or groups."

Highlight the Neighborhood

Describe the neighborhood and its attractions. Let guests know what they can expect in terms of dining, shopping, and entertainment. Mention any notable landmarks or activities nearby.

For instance, "Located in the trendy Arts District, you'll be just a short walk from eclectic cafes, boutique shops, and the famous art galleries that give the area its charm."

Use Positive and Inviting Language

Your tone should be warm and welcoming. Use positive language to make guests feel excited about the prospect of staying at your property. Words like "cozy," "luxurious," "spacious," and "inviting" can evoke the right emotions.

For example, "Unwind in the cozy reading nook, complete with a comfortable armchair and a selection of books for your enjoyment."

Address Any Potential Concerns

If there are any aspects of your property that might concern potential guests, address them upfront in a positive manner. Honesty builds trust and can prevent negative reviews.

For instance, if your property is located on a busy street, you might say, "Located in the bustling heart of the city, our home offers easy access to all major attractions. Light sleepers may want to bring earplugs for added comfort."

Conclude with a Strong Call to Action

End your description with a call to action that encourages guests to book. Reiterate what makes your property special and invite them to experience it for themselves.

For example, "Book your stay today and discover the perfect blend of comfort and convenience in the heart of the city. We look forward to hosting you!"

Writing an engaging description for your Airbnb listing involves highlighting key features, describing each room, mentioning practical details, and painting a vivid picture of the guest experience. With clear, inviting language, you can attract potential guests and ensure they feel excited and confident about booking your property.

Read the description until you make the reservation!

Price includes for one cottage, private Jacuzzi, shared garden and gazebo.

Welcome to the Loose & Moose! The top wish-listed Dreamtime A-Frame Cabin is fully equipped with a touch of luxury. Our Modern Two A Frame Cottages are nestled near Mtskheta City, Village Saguramo (25 minutes
from Tbilisi).

The space
As you entered the front door, you access the living room with kitchen and bathroom. The Kitchen provides you with everything you would need for big or small meals; including cookware, utensils, everything for BBQ. Main floor a cozy sitting are and large terrace deck with lovely 🛁 Jacuzzi on the corner of the deck.
Going upstairs - there are 2 bedrooms with one bedroom with double bed and balcony, second bedroom with two separate single beds

Guest access
Guests can access:

1. Cottage
2. Shared Garden/backyard
3. Shared Gazebo
4. Shared Terrace
5. Private Jacuzzi
6. Fast wifi
7. Everything in whole cottage
8. Cable TV
9. Washing Machine
10. Drying rack
11. Fresh linens & Towels
12. All Bathroom toiletries will be provided including hair dryer
13. BBQ and Accessories

Other things to note
In this place every corner has a story and all parts are very important for me, I built and did a hard work to make these place unique, therefore I believe you will take care and will keep it clean! Thank you and Have a lovely stay💛

Listing Description Example. Source: pricelabs.co

Utilizing Social Media and Other Platforms

Harnessing the power of social media and other online platforms can significantly boost your Airbnb listing's visibility and attract more bookings. With the right strategy, you can reach a broader audience and showcase your property's unique features effectively. Here's how to make the most of these digital tools.

Choosing the Right Platforms

Start by identifying the social media platforms that are most relevant to your target audience. Facebook, Instagram, and Pinterest are popular choices for promoting travel and accommodation. Each platform offers different ways to engage with potential guests.

Facebook is excellent for sharing detailed posts, photos, and links to your Airbnb listing. Instagram is ideal for visually showcasing your property with high-quality photos and videos. Pinterest can drive traffic to your listing through curated boards featuring your property and local attractions.

Creating Engaging Content

Your content should be engaging, informative, and visually appealing. High-quality photos and videos are essential. Showcase the best aspects of your property, highlight unique features, and include shots of local attractions to give potential guests a sense of what they can experience.

Write captivating captions that tell a story. For example, describe the comfort of your living room, the beauty of a nearby park, or the convenience of your location. Use hashtags relevant to travel and your location to increase the reach of your posts.

Consistent Posting

Consistency is key to maintaining an active presence on social media. Develop a posting schedule to ensure regular updates. This keeps your audience engaged and your property top of mind. Aim for a mix of content types, such as photos, videos, guest testimonials, and local tips.

For example, you could post a stunning photo of your living room one day, followed by a video tour of a nearby attraction the next. Regularly update your followers about availability, special offers, and any improvements or updates to your property.

Engaging with Your Audience

Interaction is crucial on social media. Respond promptly to comments, messages, and inquiries. Engage with your audience by asking questions, encouraging them to share their travel experiences, and thanking them for their feedback.

For instance, if someone comments on a photo of your property, reply with a friendly message and perhaps a tip about a local activity they might enjoy. Building relationships with potential guests can increase their likelihood of booking and recommending your property.

Leveraging Influencers and Partnerships

Collaborating with travel influencers can amplify your reach. Influencers have established audiences that trust their recommendations. Reach out to local travel bloggers or social media influencers and offer them a complimentary stay in exchange for a review or a post about your property.

Partnering with local businesses can also be beneficial. For example, collaborate with nearby restaurants, tour operators, or shops to offer exclusive discounts to your guests. This not only enhances your guests' experience but also expands your network and exposure.

Using Paid Advertising

Consider investing in paid advertising to further boost your visibility. Social media platforms offer targeted advertising options that allow you to reach specific demographics based on location, interests, and behaviors. Facebook and Instagram ads can be particularly effective.

Create compelling ads that highlight the best features of your property and include a clear call to action, such as "Book Now" or "Learn More." Monitor the performance of your ads and adjust your strategy based on the results to maximize your return on investment.

Expanding to Other Platforms

Don't limit yourself to social media. Utilize other online platforms like travel blogs, local tourism websites, and online travel communities. List your property on multiple vacation rental websites to reach a broader audience.

For example, sites like Booking.com, Vrbo, and TripAdvisor can complement your presence on Airbnb. Ensure your profiles on these platforms are complete, with detailed descriptions, high-quality photos, and up-to-date availability.

Utilizing social media and other online platforms effectively can significantly enhance your Airbnb listing's visibility and appeal. By creating engaging content, maintaining consistency, interacting with your audience, leveraging partnerships, and using targeted advertising, you can attract more guests and ensure your property stands out in a competitive market.

Chapter 8: Troubleshooting Common Issues

Handling Cancellations and No-Shows

Cancellations and no-shows can be challenging for any Airbnb host. Managing these situations effectively is essential to maintaining your property's profitability and your reputation as a reliable host. Here's how to handle cancellations and no-shows with clarity and professionalism.

Understanding Airbnb's Policies

Familiarize yourself with Airbnb's cancellation policies. Airbnb offers several options, from flexible to strict, allowing you to choose the level of flexibility you are comfortable with. Each policy has different implications for refunds and penalties, so select the one that best suits your needs and risk tolerance.

For example, a flexible policy allows guests to cancel up to 24 hours before check-in for a full refund, while a strict policy offers a 50% refund up to one week before check-in. Understanding these policies helps you manage expectations and communicate effectively with guests.

Communicating Clearly

When a guest cancels, prompt and clear communication is crucial. Acknowledge the cancellation and express your understanding. If the cancellation falls within the penalty period, explain the refund process based on your chosen policy.

For instance, you might write, "I'm sorry to hear you need to cancel your stay. As per our policy, you are eligible for a 50% refund since the cancellation is within one week of your check-in date. Airbnb will process the refund, and you should see it on your account soon."

Rebooking the Dates

Once a cancellation occurs, update your calendar immediately to make the dates available for other potential guests. Consider adjusting your pricing slightly to attract last-minute bookings. Use Airbnb's tools to boost visibility, such as instant booking or last-minute deals, to fill the vacancy quickly.

Handling No-Shows

A no-show occurs when a guest fails to arrive without canceling their booking. This situation can be frustrating, but having a clear plan in place can help you manage it smoothly.

If a guest does not show up by the expected check-in time, send a polite message to check if they are still coming. For example, "Hi [Guest's Name], we noticed you haven't checked in yet. Please let us know if you're still planning to arrive or if there have been any changes to your plans."

If there's no response and the guest still doesn't arrive, you are typically entitled to keep the payment according to your cancellation policy. Document the no-show in Airbnb's system to protect yourself in case of any disputes.

Preventing Future Issues

While cancellations and no-shows can't always be avoided, there are steps you can take to minimize their occurrence. Clear and detailed communication before the booking can help set expectations and reduce misunderstandings. Send reminders about the booking and check-in procedures as the date approaches.

For example, "We're looking forward to hosting you! Just a reminder, check-in is from 3 PM onwards. Please let us know your estimated arrival time."

Offering Flexibility When Possible

In some cases, offering a degree of flexibility can enhance guest satisfaction and protect your reputation. If a guest needs to cancel due to unforeseen circumstances, consider offering to rebook their stay for a future date if your schedule allows. This gesture can turn a potentially negative experience into a positive one.

For example, "I'm sorry to hear about your situation. While our policy does not allow for a refund at this time, I'd be happy to offer you a chance to rebook for another date within the next six months, subject to availability."

Leveraging Reviews and Feedback

Encourage guests to leave reviews even if their plans change. Positive reviews about your understanding and professionalism in handling cancellations can enhance your reputation. Responding to any feedback about the booking process can also provide insights into how you might improve your handling of cancellations and no-shows.

For instance, "Thank you for your feedback. We strive to be as accommodating as possible and appreciate your understanding regarding our cancellation policy."

Handling cancellations and no-shows effectively involves clear communication, prompt action to rebook dates, and a proactive approach to minimize future occurrences. By being understanding and flexible, while also protecting your interests, you can manage these situations smoothly and maintain a positive relationship with your guests.

Dealing with Difficult Guests: Strategies for Resolution

Handling difficult guests is an inevitable part of being an Airbnb host. The key to managing these situations is to remain calm, communicate effectively, and find solutions that address both your needs and those of your guests. Here are strategies to help you resolve conflicts and maintain a positive hosting experience.

Stay Calm and Professional

When faced with a difficult guest, it's crucial to stay calm and professional. Reacting emotionally can escalate the situation and make it harder to reach a resolution. Take a deep breath, listen to the guest's concerns, and approach the issue with a problem-solving mindset.

For instance, if a guest complains about the cleanliness of the property, respond with, "I'm sorry to hear that you're unhappy with the cleanliness. Let's discuss what can be done to address this issue immediately."

Listen and Understand

Active listening is essential when dealing with complaints or conflicts. Allow the guest to fully explain their concerns without interrupting. This shows respect and helps you understand the root of the problem. Once they've finished, summarize what you've heard to ensure you've understood correctly.

For example, "I understand that you're upset because the Wi-Fi isn't working. Let me see what I can do to fix this for you right away."

Address the Issue Promptly

Timely action can prevent small issues from becoming larger problems. If the issue can be resolved quickly, such as fixing a broken appliance or providing additional supplies, do so as soon as possible. Keeping the guest informed about the steps you're taking can help reassure them.

For example, "I've contacted a technician, and they'll be here within the hour to repair the Wi-Fi. Thank you for your patience."

Offer Solutions and Alternatives

When resolving conflicts, offering multiple solutions can give guests a sense of control and satisfaction. If an immediate fix isn't possible, suggest alternatives that can mitigate the inconvenience. This might include offering a partial refund, an extra night's stay, or a small gift as a gesture of goodwill.

For instance, "Unfortunately, the technician won't be able to fix the issue until tomorrow. In the meantime, I'd like to offer you a complimentary breakfast at a nearby café for the inconvenience."

Set Clear Boundaries

While it's important to be accommodating, it's also necessary to set clear boundaries to protect your property and ensure mutual respect. If a guest's behavior is unacceptable, such as violating house rules or being disruptive, communicate your expectations firmly and politely.

For example, "We have a strict no-smoking policy inside the house. If you continue to smoke indoors, I will need to involve Airbnb to resolve this issue."

Document Everything

Keep detailed records of all communications with difficult guests. This includes messages, emails, and notes about phone calls or in-person interactions. Documenting everything can be crucial if the issue escalates and requires mediation by Airbnb or legal action.

For example, "Following up on our conversation earlier, I've noted that you expressed concerns about the heating system. I've arranged for a technician to visit tomorrow morning."

Seek Mediation from Airbnb

If you're unable to resolve the issue directly with the guest, don't hesitate to seek help from Airbnb. The platform offers mediation services that can assist in finding a fair resolution. Provide Airbnb with all relevant documentation and evidence to support your case.

For instance, if a guest demands an unreasonable refund after causing damage, Airbnb can review the situation and determine an appropriate course of action.

Learn and Adapt

Each difficult situation is an opportunity to learn and improve. Reflect on what happened, what worked, and what didn't. Use this experience to update your house rules, improve your property, or adjust your communication strategies to prevent similar issues in the future.

For example, if multiple guests have had trouble with the same appliance, consider replacing it with a more reliable model and providing clearer instructions for its use.

Dealing with difficult guests requires patience, clear communication, and a proactive approach to problem-solving. By staying calm, listening, and addressing issues promptly, you can manage conflicts effectively and maintain a positive relationship with your guests.

Maintenance and Repairs: Keeping Your Space in Top Shape

Maintaining your Airbnb in top condition is essential for providing a great guest experience and protecting your investment. Regular maintenance and prompt repairs ensure that everything functions smoothly and looks inviting. Here's how to keep your space in excellent shape.

Regular Inspections

Perform regular inspections of your property to catch potential issues early. Check all areas of the house, including plumbing, electrical systems, appliances, and furniture. Look for signs of wear and tear, leaks, and other problems that might need attention.

For example, inspect the bathroom for any signs of mold, check the kitchen appliances to ensure they are working properly, and test all lights and electrical outlets.

Seasonal Maintenance

Different seasons bring different maintenance needs. Prepare your property accordingly to ensure it remains in good condition year-round. In the spring and summer, focus on outdoor maintenance, such as cleaning gutters, checking for roof damage, and maintaining the garden or yard.

In the fall and winter, ensure the heating system is working efficiently, check windows and doors for drafts, and make sure any outdoor pipes are insulated to prevent freezing.

Quick Response to Repairs

When a guest reports an issue, respond promptly to address it. Quick repairs not only keep your property in good condition but also show guests that you care about their comfort and satisfaction. Establish a network of reliable contractors and service providers who can help with repairs as needed.

For example, if a guest reports a leaking faucet, arrange for a plumber to fix it as soon as possible. Keep a list of emergency contacts for situations that require immediate attention, such as electrical problems or significant water damage.

Routine Cleaning and Upkeep

Regular cleaning is crucial for maintaining your property's appearance and hygiene. Beyond the standard cleaning between guest stays, schedule deep cleanings periodically. This includes tasks like carpet cleaning, washing windows, and scrubbing grout.

Also, pay attention to less obvious areas such as air vents, behind appliances, and inside cabinets. Regular upkeep ensures that your property remains fresh and appealing to guests.

Upgrading and Replacing Items

Over time, some items in your property will need to be replaced or upgraded. Keep an eye on the condition of furniture, linens, and appliances. Investing in high-quality replacements can enhance the guest experience and reduce the frequency of future replacements.

For example, if the sofa in the living room starts to show significant wear, consider replacing it with a durable, comfortable option that matches the room's decor.

Landscaping and Exterior Care

The exterior of your property is the first thing guests see, so maintaining curb appeal is important. Regularly mow the lawn, trim bushes, and clean outdoor areas. Ensure pathways are clear and safe, and check exterior lighting to make sure it works properly.

In winter, keep walkways free of snow and ice to prevent accidents. A well-maintained exterior creates a welcoming impression and adds to the overall guest experience.

Keeping a Maintenance Log

Maintain a log of all maintenance and repair activities. This helps you track what has been done and when, making it easier to schedule future maintenance and identify recurring issues. A detailed log can also be helpful if you ever need to provide maintenance history to guests or potential buyers.

For example, record the dates of HVAC servicing, appliance repairs, and any major upgrades or replacements. Include details about the work done and contact information for the service providers.

Budgeting for Maintenance

Set aside a portion of your rental income for maintenance and repairs. This ensures you have funds available for both routine upkeep and unexpected issues. Having a budget in place can help you manage expenses without compromising the quality of your property.

For instance, allocate a percentage of your monthly earnings to a maintenance fund, which can be used for both minor fixes and larger projects.

Maintaining your Airbnb in top shape requires regular inspections, prompt repairs, and ongoing care. By staying proactive and organized, you can ensure your property remains appealing and functional, providing a great experience for your guests and protecting your investment.

Area	Maintenance Checks
Kitchen	☐ Faucet, drain, and kitchen sprayer checks ☐ Appliance checks: fridge/freezer, oven ☐ Cabinet door and handle checks
Bathrooms	☐ Toilet, faucet, and drain checks ☐ Inspection for mold or leaks in showers
General Interior	☐ Under-bed and rug cleaning ☐ Water heater checks ☐ Pest and insect infestation checks ☐ Laundry vent and bulb checks ☐ Fan, TV, furnace filter checks ☐ Window, smoke detector, fire extinguisher, fireplace checks
General Exterior	☐ Pre-winter gutter cleaning ☐ Bi-annual roof inspections ☐ Tree and lawn checks ☐ Hot tub checks ☐ Structural damage checks ☐ Identification of important locations: water and gas shut-off, breaker box

Maintenance Checklist Example. Source: awning.com.

Chapter 9: Legal and Financial Considerations

Understanding Local Regulations: Compliance is Key

Operating an Airbnb requires more than just preparing your property and welcoming guests. It is crucial to understand and comply with local regulations to avoid legal issues and fines. Compliance ensures that your business runs smoothly and that you maintain a good standing within your community. Here's how to navigate local regulations effectively.

Researching Local Laws

Begin by researching the specific laws and regulations that apply to short-term rentals in your area. These can vary significantly from one location to another, so it's essential to know the rules that pertain to your city, county, or state. Check with local government websites, housing departments, or legal advisors to get accurate and up-to-date information.

For example, some cities require a special permit or license to operate a short-term rental, while others might have zoning laws that restrict where these rentals can be located.

Understanding Zoning Regulations

Zoning laws dictate how properties in certain areas can be used. Make sure your property is zoned for short-term rentals. If it's not, you might need to apply for a zoning variance or select a different property that meets zoning requirements.

Contact your local zoning office to confirm whether your property complies with these regulations. This step is crucial to avoid penalties and ensure that your rental operation is legal.

Registering Your Property

Many jurisdictions require short-term rental operators to register their properties. Registration can involve submitting an application, paying a fee, and providing details about your property and its use as a rental. Keep records of your registration and any related correspondence for future reference.

For instance, New York City requires hosts to register with the Office of Special Enforcement and comply with various safety and operational standards.

Adhering to Safety Standards

Safety regulations are designed to protect both hosts and guests. Ensure your property meets local safety standards, which might include having smoke detectors, carbon monoxide detectors, fire extinguishers, and clear emergency exits. Regularly inspect and maintain these safety features to stay compliant.

For example, San Francisco mandates that short-term rentals must comply with building and fire safety codes, and hosts must provide proof of compliance during inspections.

Paying Taxes

Understand the tax obligations associated with running a short-term rental. This can include occupancy taxes, sales taxes, and income taxes. Some jurisdictions require hosts to collect and remit these taxes on behalf of their guests. Familiarize yourself with these requirements and set up a system to ensure timely and accurate tax payments.

For example, in many places, Airbnb collects and remits occupancy taxes on behalf of hosts, but you might still be responsible for reporting and paying other taxes related to your rental income.

Respecting Neighborhood Rules

Beyond government regulations, be aware of any rules set by homeowners associations (HOAs) or neighborhood groups. These rules can impact your ability to operate a short-term rental and might include restrictions on noise, parking, or the number of guests allowed.

For example, some HOAs have strict rules against short-term rentals, so it's important to review your HOA's covenants, conditions, and restrictions (CC&Rs) before listing your property.

Handling Guest Information

Some local regulations require hosts to keep records of their guests, including names, contact information, and the duration of their stay. Ensure you understand these requirements and comply with any record-keeping mandates. This information can be crucial in case of legal inquiries or compliance audits.

For instance, in Los Angeles, hosts must keep guest records for three years and make them available to the city upon request.

Seeking Legal Advice

If you're unsure about any regulations or how to comply with them, seek legal advice. A lawyer with experience in short-term rentals can provide guidance specific to your situation and help you navigate complex legal requirements.

Compliance with local regulations is essential for operating a successful and legal Airbnb. By thoroughly understanding and adhering to these rules, you can protect yourself from fines, legal issues, and potential shutdowns, ensuring a sustainable and profitable rental business.

Managing Finances: Budgeting and Record-Keeping

Effective financial management is critical for the success of your Airbnb business. Budgeting and meticulous record-keeping help you understand your expenses, maximize your profits, and ensure compliance with tax regulations. Here's how to manage your finances efficiently.

Creating a Budget

Start by creating a detailed budget that includes all potential expenses and income sources. Your budget should cover initial setup costs, ongoing expenses, and projected income. This helps you plan ahead and avoid unexpected financial shortfalls.

Initial Setup Costs: These are one-time expenses such as furnishing your property, purchasing appliances, and making any necessary renovations or upgrades. Include costs for marketing your listing, professional photography, and initial supplies like linens and toiletries.

Ongoing Expenses: These include utilities, cleaning services, maintenance, insurance, and any fees associated with your property management software or Airbnb itself. Don't forget to budget for periodic deep cleaning and replacement of worn-out items.

Projected Income: Estimate your monthly income based on your expected occupancy rate and nightly rates. Factor in seasonal variations and any special events that might affect demand in your area.

Tracking Income and Expenses

Maintaining accurate records of all income and expenses is essential for understanding your business's financial health and for tax purposes. Use a dedicated system for tracking your finances, whether it's a spreadsheet, accounting software, or a specialized property management tool.

Income Tracking: Record each booking, including the dates, guest details, and total amount paid. Include any additional income from services you offer, such as airport pickups or guided tours.

Expense Tracking: Keep detailed records of all expenses. Categorize them for easier analysis and tax reporting. Common categories might include utilities, cleaning, repairs, supplies, marketing, and professional services.

Managing Cash Flow

Cash flow management ensures you have enough funds to cover your expenses at all times. Monitor your cash flow regularly to identify any potential issues early.

Timely Payments: Ensure you receive payments from Airbnb promptly and that your payment methods are set up correctly. Schedule your expenses to align with your income, paying bills on time to avoid late fees and maintain good relationships with your service providers.

Emergency Fund: Set aside a portion of your income to create an emergency fund. This fund can cover unexpected expenses such as urgent repairs, cancellations, or periods of low occupancy.

Keeping Financial Records

Accurate and organized financial records are crucial for managing your Airbnb and preparing for tax season. Develop a system for storing and organizing your financial documents.

Receipts and Invoices: Keep digital or physical copies of all receipts and invoices. Organize them by category and date to make retrieval easy.

Bank Statements: Regularly review your bank statements to ensure all transactions are accounted for and to identify any discrepancies.

Tax Documents: Keep all relevant tax documents, including any forms from Airbnb and receipts for deductible expenses. This will make tax preparation easier and help you avoid issues with tax authorities.

Preparing for Taxes

Understanding your tax obligations is critical. Different regions have varying tax laws regarding short-term rentals, so it's essential to stay informed and compliant.

Income Tax: Report your Airbnb income as part of your personal or business income. Deduct eligible expenses to reduce your taxable income. Common deductions include mortgage interest, property insurance, utilities, cleaning fees, and repairs.

Occupancy Tax: Some areas require you to collect and remit occupancy taxes from your guests. Check your local regulations to ensure compliance. Airbnb may handle this in some jurisdictions, but you need to verify and possibly register with local tax authorities.

Professional Advice: Consider hiring an accountant or tax advisor with experience in short-term rentals. They can provide guidance tailored to your situation, help you maximize deductions, and ensure you comply with all tax laws.

Regular Financial Reviews

Conduct regular reviews of your financial performance. Compare your actual income and expenses to your budget to identify any variances and adjust your plans accordingly.

Monthly Reviews: Review your income and expenses monthly to ensure you stay on track. Look for patterns or anomalies that need attention.

Annual Reviews: At the end of each year, conduct a comprehensive review of your financial performance. Use this review to plan for the upcoming year, adjusting your budget and strategies as needed.

Effective budgeting and record-keeping are foundational to the success of your Airbnb business. By staying organized and proactive with your finances, you can ensure a smooth operation, maximize your profitability, and maintain compliance with tax regulations.

Insurance and Liability: Protecting Your Investment

Running an Airbnb comes with unique risks, making it crucial to have the right insurance and liability coverage. Proper protection safeguards your property and finances, giving you peace of mind. Here's how to ensure your investment is adequately protected.

Understanding Airbnb's Host Liability Insurance Program

Airbnb offers two primary forms of coverage for hosts: the Host Guarantee and Host Protection Insurance. It's essential to understand what these coverages provide and their limitations.

Host Guarantee: This program provides coverage for damages to your property up to $1 million. However, it does not cover everything. For instance, it excludes personal liability, cash and securities, and certain types of property damage like wear and tear.

Host Protection Insurance: This covers liability claims up to $1 million per occurrence. It protects against claims of bodily injury or property damage brought by guests or others. However, it doesn't cover things like intentional acts or injuries that occur in common areas outside your listing, such as lobbies or shared spaces.

While these programs provide a layer of protection, they may not cover all potential risks, making additional insurance necessary.

Obtaining Homeowners or Landlord Insurance

Traditional homeowners insurance typically doesn't cover short-term rentals. Therefore, if you plan to host guests regularly, you might need a landlord insurance policy or a specialized short-term rental policy.

Landlord Insurance: This type of policy is designed for rental properties and usually covers the building, any outbuildings, and liability. It's more suitable for long-term rentals but can be adapted with additional endorsements for short-term rentals.

Short-Term Rental Insurance: Some insurance companies offer policies specifically for short-term rentals. These policies cover the unique risks associated with hosting guests, such as property damage caused by guests, liability for guest injuries, and loss of income due to cancellations.

When shopping for insurance, be transparent with your insurer about how often you plan to rent out your property and any specific concerns you have.

Additional Coverage Options

Depending on your circumstances, you might consider additional coverage options to enhance your protection.

Personal Property Coverage: If you provide high-value items for guest use, such as electronics, artwork, or expensive furnishings, ensure they are covered under your policy. Some policies might limit coverage for personal belongings, so verify and adjust as needed.

Umbrella Insurance: This provides additional liability coverage beyond the limits of your primary policies. It's especially useful if you have substantial assets to protect or if your property is frequently rented.

Business Interruption Insurance: If your rental income is a significant part of your earnings, this coverage can compensate for lost income if your property becomes uninhabitable due to a covered event, such as a fire or natural disaster.

Implementing Risk Management Practices

Insurance is a critical safety net, but implementing risk management practices can help prevent incidents and minimize claims.

Guest Screening: Use Airbnb's guest review system to screen potential guests. Look for guests with positive reviews and verify their identity through Airbnb's verification process.

House Rules: Clearly communicate your house rules and expectations to guests. This includes policies on smoking, pets, parties, and maximum occupancy. Display these rules prominently in your property and in your listing description.

Safety Features: Equip your property with essential safety features such as smoke detectors, carbon monoxide detectors, fire extinguishers, and first aid kits. Regularly check and maintain these devices.

Security Measures: Consider installing security cameras in common areas (while respecting privacy laws) and using smart locks to enhance security. Ensure guests know how to use these features and feel secure during their stay.

Handling Claims and Disputes

Despite precautions, incidents can still occur. Knowing how to handle claims and disputes efficiently is crucial.

Documentation: Keep detailed records of your property's condition, including photos and videos, before and after each guest's stay. This documentation is invaluable if you need to file a claim.

Reporting Incidents: Report any incidents to your insurance provider and Airbnb as soon as possible. Provide all necessary documentation and cooperate fully with their investigations.

Mediation: If a dispute arises with a guest, try to resolve it amicably through communication. If this isn't possible, use

Airbnb's Resolution Center or seek mediation through your insurance provider.

Having the right insurance and liability coverage, combined with effective risk management practices, ensures that your Airbnb investment is well-protected. This approach not only safeguards your property but also provides a secure and trustworthy environment for your guests.

Conclusion

As we reach the end of this journey through the essentials of Airbnb hosting, we hope you feel more empowered, prepared, and inspired to create exceptional experiences for your guests. This book has covered a wide range of topics, from preparing your property and setting the right price to mastering guest communication and understanding local regulations. Each chapter has been designed to equip you with practical strategies and insights to help you stand out in the world of Airbnb hosting.

At its core, this book is about more than just making extra income; it's about building a fulfilling and successful hosting experience. The Airbnb platform offers hosts the chance to connect with people from around the world, to share the unique qualities of their space, and to create a welcoming environment that guests will remember long after their stay. By focusing on preparation, attentiveness, and genuine hospitality, you're not only creating a memorable experience for others but also cultivating a rewarding venture for yourself.

Hosting on Airbnb is a dynamic and evolving journey. Every guest brings new opportunities to learn, adapt, and improve. With the knowledge and tips you've gained from this book, you're now equipped to handle the challenges, embrace the opportunities, and create a thriving Airbnb listing. Remember that the best hosts are those who continually seek ways to enhance their offering, listen to guest feedback, and maintain a passion for hospitality. Your dedication to these principles will set you apart and ensure lasting success in the Airbnb community.

As you apply the insights and strategies you've learned here, remember that hosting is ultimately about creating connections, building trust, and providing a space where guests feel welcome and valued. Each stay you host has the potential to make a positive impact, both for your guests and for you. So, take pride in what you've created, continue to refine your approach, and let each experience inspire you to grow even further.

Here's to your success as an exceptional Airbnb host. May your hosting journey be filled with rewarding experiences, happy guests, and countless opportunities to make a difference—one stay at a time. Thank you for choosing this path, and may your Airbnb endeavors bring you lasting fulfillment and success.

Dear Reader,

I hope you found this book insightful and valuable.

Your feedback is invaluable to me. If you enjoyed this book, I would appreciate it if you could take a moment to leave a review on the reading apps and platforms.

Thank you for your support, and I wish you all the best.

Kind regards,
Ghazwan

About the Author

Ghazwan is a passionate entrepreneur and business strategist dedicated to helping individuals and organizations achieve their full potential with a deep understanding of modern businesses' challenges and opportunities.

With a Master's degree in Computer and Systems Sciences from Stockholm University, specializing in eService design, requirement engineering, and business process management, he is equipped to innovate cutting-edge solutions.

He believes in the power of collaboration and lifelong learning, and his mission is to empower people to reach their goals and positively impact the world.

www.ingramcontent.com/pod-product-compliance
Lightning Source LLC
Chambersburg PA
CBHW071510220526
45472CB00003B/969